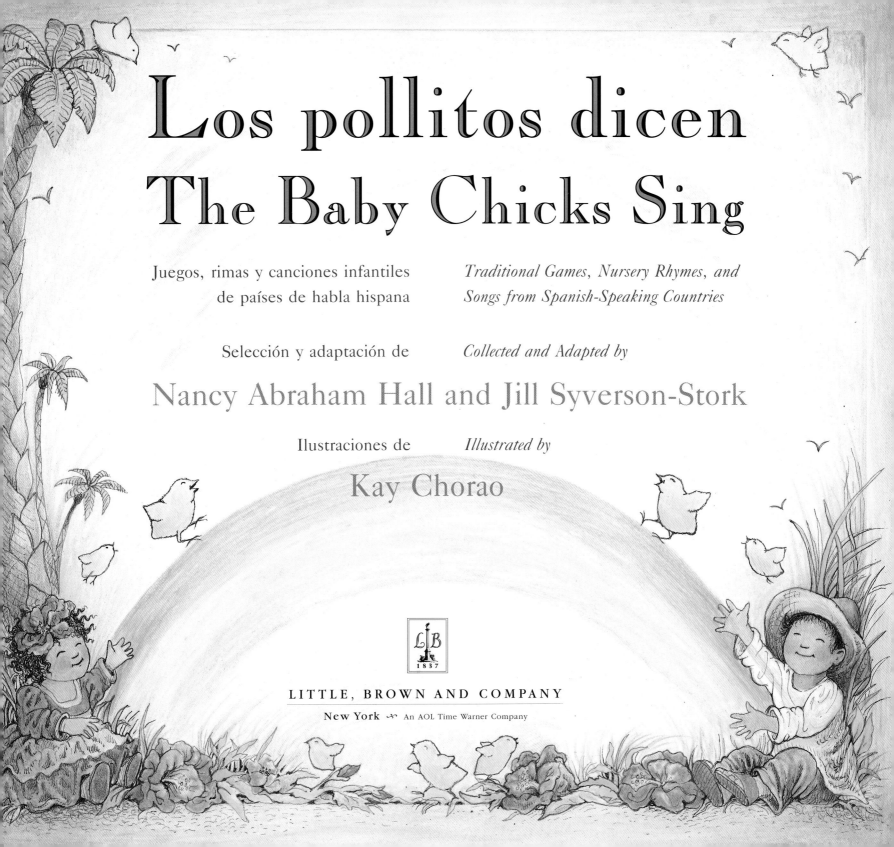

Los pollitos dicen
The Baby Chicks Sing

Juegos, rimas y canciones infantiles
de países de habla hispana

Traditional Games, Nursery Rhymes, and
Songs from Spanish-Speaking Countries

Selección y adaptación de

Collected and Adapted by

Nancy Abraham Hall and Jill Syverson-Stork

Ilustraciones de

Illustrated by

Kay Chorao

LITTLE, BROWN AND COMPANY

New York · An AOL Time Warner Company

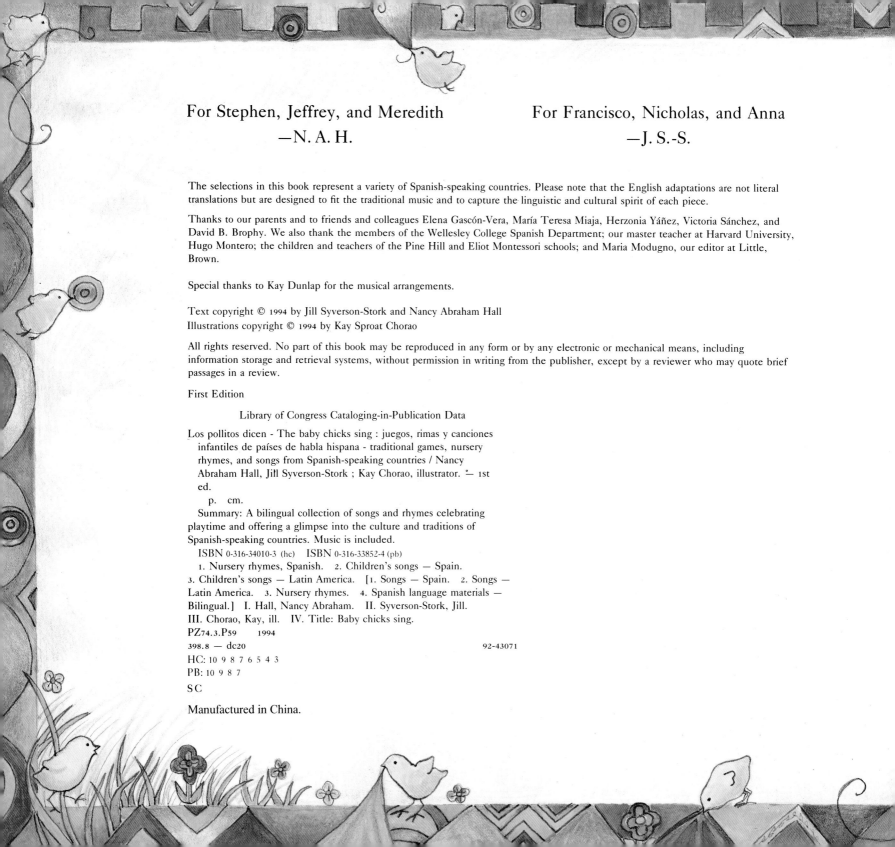

For Stephen, Jeffrey, and Meredith
—N. A. H.

For Francisco, Nicholas, and Anna
—J. S.-S.

The selections in this book represent a variety of Spanish-speaking countries. Please note that the English adaptations are not literal translations but are designed to fit the traditional music and to capture the linguistic and cultural spirit of each piece.

Thanks to our parents and to friends and colleagues Elena Gascón-Vera, María Teresa Miaja, Herzonia Yáñez, Victoria Sánchez, and David B. Brophy. We also thank the members of the Wellesley College Spanish Department; our master teacher at Harvard University, Hugo Montero; the children and teachers of the Pine Hill and Eliot Montessori schools; and Maria Modugno, our editor at Little, Brown.

Special thanks to Kay Dunlap for the musical arrangements.

Text copyright © 1994 by Jill Syverson-Stork and Nancy Abraham Hall
Illustrations copyright © 1994 by Kay Sproat Chorao

First Edition

Library of Congress Cataloging-in-Publication Data

Los pollitos dicen - The baby chicks sing : juegos, rimas y canciones
infantiles de países de habla hispana - traditional games, nursery
rhymes, and songs from Spanish-speaking countries / Nancy
Abraham Hall, Jill Syverson-Stork ; Kay Chorao, illustrator. — 1st
ed.
p.   cm.
Summary: A bilingual collection of songs and rhymes celebrating
playtime and offering a glimpse into the culture and traditions of
Spanish-speaking countries. Music is included.
ISBN 0-316-34010-3 (hc)   ISBN 0-316-33852-4 (pb)
1. Nursery rhymes, Spanish.   2. Children's songs — Spain.
3. Children's songs — Latin America.   [1. Songs — Spain.   2. Songs —
Latin America.   3. Nursery rhymes.   4. Spanish language materials —
Bilingual.]   I. Hall, Nancy Abraham.   II. Syverson-Stork, Jill.
III. Chorao, Kay, ill.   IV. Title: Baby chicks sing.
PZ74.3.P59   1994
398.8 — dc20   92-43071
HC: 10 9 8 7 6 5 4 3
PB: 10 9 8 7
S C

Manufactured in China.

Índice

Contents

Los pollitos dicen   The Baby Chicks Sing

Con brío   Brightly

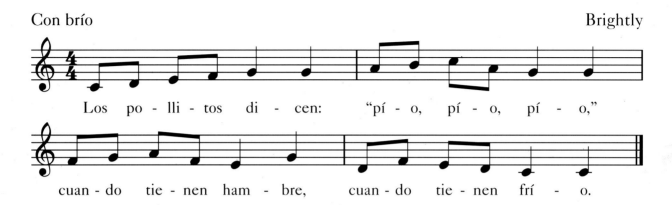

Los po - lli - tos di - cen: "pí - o, pí - o, pí - o,"

cuan - do tie - nen ham - bre, cuan - do tie - nen frí - o.

La gallina busca
el maíz y el trigo;
les da la comida,
y les presta abrigo.

Bajo sus dos alas,
acurrucaditos,
hasta el otro día
duermen los pollitos.

The baby chicks are saying,
"Peep, peep, peep."
It means they're cold and hungry;
It means they need some sleep.

The mother hen finds corn;
She also finds them wheat.
She gathers them together,
And she makes sure they eat.

Then with her wings she cuddles them
And gives her chicks a hug;
All through the night she covers them
And keeps them warm and snug.

La casa del conejo

The Bunny's House

Es la casa del conejo
y el conejo no está aquí;
ha salido esta mañana
y no ha vuelto por aquí.

¡Ay! ¡ay! ¡ay! ¡ay!
El conejo ya está aquí.
Escoge a la niña (niño)
que te guste más a ti.

This is the bunny's house,
But the bunny isn't home.
He went out this morning;
He went out to roam.

Oh! Oh! Oh! Oh!
The bunny is back to rest.
Now choose the little girl (boy)
That you like best.

6

Un niño o una niña, "el conejo," se queda fuera de la rueda, para luego entrar al centro y escoger al que lo va a sustituir.

The child who is "the bunny" stands outside the circle, then enters to choose a replacement.

Arre, caballito — Giddyup, Little Pony

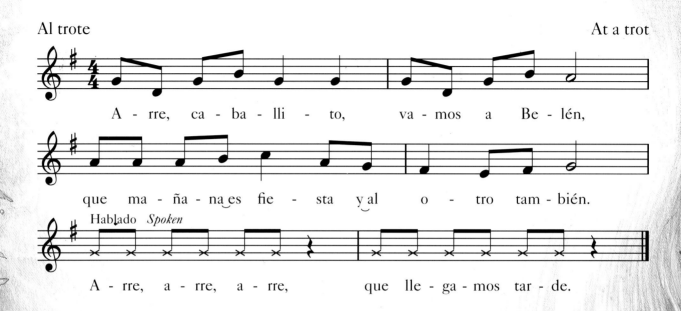

Al trote — At a trot

A - rre, ca - ba - lli - to, va - mos a Be - lén,

que ma - ña - na_es fie - sta y al o - tro tam - bién.

Hablado *Spoken*

A - rre, a - rre, a - rre, que lle - ga - mos tar - de.

Giddyup, little pony,
To Bethlehem we go.
Tomorrow and the next day
Are holidays, you know.

[Spoken:]
Giddyup, giddyup, giddyup,
We can't be late, oh no!

Se coloca al niño sobre la rodilla y se mueve la pierna de arriba a abajo.
Bounce the child on your knee.

8

Caballito blanco   Little White Pony

Con gracia   Lightly

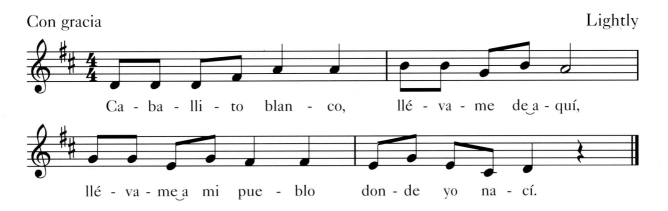

Ca - ba - lli - to blan - co, llé - va - me de a - quí,

llé - va - me a mi pue - blo don - de yo na - cí.

Tengo, tengo, tengo,
tú no tienes nada,
tengo tres ovejas
en una cabaña.

There's something, something special,
Waiting there for me:
Fine sheep in a thatched hut,
One . . . two . . . three!

Una me da leche,
otra me da lana,
otra mantequilla
para la semana.

One sheep gives me milk to drink,
Another gives me wool,
Another gives me butter,
A whole week's full.

Little white pony,
Let's gallop away.
Take me to my hometown,
My birthplace, today.

9

Un elefante   One Elephant

Un e - le - fan - te se ba - lan - cea - ba

so - bre la te - la de u - na a - ra - ña;

co - mo ve - í - a que re - sis - tí - a,

fue a lla - mar a___ o - tro e - le - fan - te.

Dos elefantes se balanceaban
sobre la tela de una araña;
como veían que resistía,
fueron a llamar a otro elefante.

Tres elefantes . . .

One huge elephant
Balancing carefully
On the web of a spider.
When he saw the web was strong,
He called another elephant to come along.

Two huge elephants
Balancing carefully
On the web of a spider.
When they saw the web was strong,
They called another elephant to come along.

Three huge elephants . . .

La panaderita   The Little Bread Girl

Dulcemente   Sweetly

A la en - tra - da del pue - blo y a la sa - li - da, ___

___ hay u - na pa - na - de - ra, pa - na - de - ri -

ta, pa - na - de - ri - ta. ¡Qué pa - na - de - ra lin -

da y chi - qui - ta, qué pa - na - de - ra, pa - na - de - ri - ta!

Al besarla le ha dicho hoy, su abuelita:
"Eres sabrosa, niña,
como la miga, como la miga."
¡Qué panadera, linda y chiquita,
que panadera, panaderita!

12

At the entrance and exit to our little town,
There is a pretty young girl
Who is known all around:
Our little bread girl.
Oh, what a bread girl, sweet little bread girl;
Oh, what a bread girl, sweet little bread girl.

When she kissed her this morning,
Her grandmother said,
"You are scrumptious and tasty
Like freshly baked bread:
Our little bread girl."
Oh, what a bread girl, sweet little bread girl;
Oh, what a bread girl, sweet little bread girl.

Tortillitas   Little Corn Cakes

Sencillamente   Simply

Tor - ti - lli - tas   pa - ra ma - má,   tor - ti - lli - tas   pa - ra pa - pá,

las que - ma - di - tas   pa - ra - ma - má,   las   bo - ni - tas   pa - ra pa - pá.

Corn cakes for Mama,
Corn cakes for Papa,
Crispy ones for Mama,
Pretty ones for Papa.

Se bate palmas mientras se canta.
Clap hands as you pretend to make tortillas.

14

Chocolate   Hot Chocolate

¡Uno . . . dos . . . tres . . . cho!
¡Uno . . . dos . . . tres . . . co!
¡Uno . . . dos . . . tres . . . la!
¡Uno . . . dos . . . tres . . . te!
¡Bate, bate, chocolate!

One . . . *two* . . . *three* . . . *hot!*
One . . . *two* . . . *three* . . . *chocolate!*
One . . . *two* . . . *three* . . . *hot!*
One . . . *two* . . . *three* . . . *chocolate!*
Whip it up, hot chocolate!

Mientras cantan, los niños fingen frotar un batidor entre las manos para
batir un tazón de chocolate con leche.
As they chant, children pretend to rotate a wooden whisk between the palms of their hands
in order to whip a cup of hot chocolate to a froth.

15

Arroz con leche   Rice Pudding with Milk

Festivamente   Playfully

A - rroz con le - che, me quie-ro ca - sar con un me - xi - ca - no que

se - pa can - tar. El hi - jo del rey me man-da un pa - pel, me

man - da de - cir que me ca - se con él. Con és - te sí, con

és - te no, con és - te me - ro me ca - so yo.

Rice pudding with milk,
I'd like a gold ring
From a Mexican boy
Who knows how to sing.

The son of the king
Has sent me a letter
To say, as my husband,
That he would be better.

With this one yes,
With this one no,
Eeney, meeney, miney, mo!

Se sientan los niños y pasa una niña cantando. Ésta señala a un niño que
sale a bailar con ella.
A girl strolls by a group of seated children and chooses a boy to dance with her.

17

Al corro de la patata   Ring Around the Potato

Acompasado   Rhythmically

Al co-rro de la pa-ta-ta, co-me-re-mos en-sa-la-da co-mo

Hablado *Spoken*

co-men los se-ño-res, na-ran-ji-tas y li-mo-nes. ¡A-chu-

pé, a-chu-pé! Sen-ta-di-ta me que-dé.

Ring around the potato,
Eating salad greens with tomato
Like gentle people eat,
Eating citrus fruits so sweet.
To the ground, to the ground
We all fall down!

18

Los niños giran en rueda y al decir el último verso, todos se sientan.
The children hold hands and go around in a circle, then all sit down.

Bajen la piñata   Lower the Piñata

Bajen la piñata,
bájenla un tantito,
que le den de palos
poquito a poquito.

Lower the piñata,
Lower it a bit,
So that they can give it
Another little hit!

20

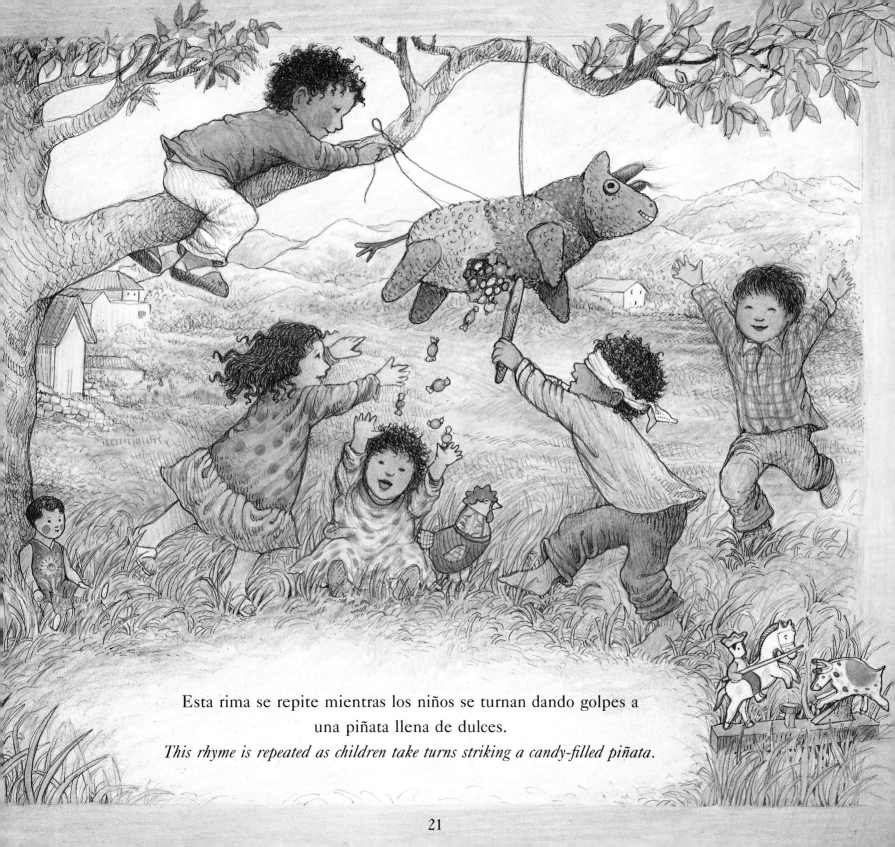

Esta rima se repite mientras los niños se turnan dando golpes a
una piñata llena de dulces.
This rhyme is repeated as children take turns striking a candy-filled piñata.

A la víbora de la mar   Like a Snake in the Sea

Con rapidez   Quickly

A la ví - bo - ra, ví - bo - ra de la mar, de la mar,

por a - quí pue - den pa - sar; los de a de-lan - te co - rren mu - cho, y

los de a - trás se que - da - rán, ¡tras, tras, tras!

Like a snake, like a snake,
Swimming in the sea, in the sea,
Through this bridge pass rapidly;
Those in front will go through fast,
And those in back will go through
Last, last, last!

Los pescaditos   The Little Fishes

Con fluidez   Fluidly

Los pes - ca - di - tos an - dan en el a - gua, na-dan, na-dan,

na-dan, vue-lan, vue-lan, vue-lan. Son chi-qui - ti - tos, chi-qui-ti - tos, chi-qui-

ti - tos, vue-lan, vue-lan, vue - lan, na-dan, na-dan, na - dan.

The little fishes they move through the water,
Swimming, swimming, swimming,
Flying, flying, flying.

They're very little, very little, very little,
Flying, flying, flying,
Swimming, swimming, swimming.

La reina de los mares   The Queen of the Sea

Con desenvoltura   Jauntily

En el puen-te ma-ri - ne - ro hay u-na ni-ña brin-

can - do, con su le-tra lo que di - ce:

"Soy la rei - na de los ma - res."

"Soy la reina de los mares,
ustedes lo van a ver,
tiro mi pañuelo al suelo
y lo vuelvo a recoger."

Si la cosa no se acaba,
la culpa la tienes tú,
por andar de parrandera
con tu vestidito azul.

[Hablado:]
Uno, dos y tres,
sota, caballo y rey.

Out upon the sailors' bridge
A girl is jumping happily,
As she jumps she sings this song:
"I'm the queen of the sea."

"I'm the queen of the sea,
Watch and know that when
I drop my hankie on the floor,
I will pick it up again!"

If we do not finish,
We will put the blame on you,
So busy flaunting your new dress,
That very fancy dress of blue.

[Spoken:]
One, two, three,
Out!

Canción para jugar a la cuerda. Se tira un objeto al suelo que luego se recoje.
A jump rope song in which an object is dropped and recovered by the singer.

El sereno   The Watchman

cin - co, las seis, las sie - te, las o - cho, las nue - ve, las

diez. Se - re - no que can - ta, dime qué ho - ra es.

The watchman who patrols my street
Has a voice that's very sweet.
When he sings the time of day,
Only he can sing that way.

Oh, watchman, oh, watchman,
What time is it please?
It's already one o'clock,
Two o'clock, three.
It's four o'clock, five o'clock,
Six, seven, eight.
It's nine o'clock, ten.
Is it early or late?

27

Duérmete, niñito   Go to Sleep, Dear Child

Con ternura   Tenderly

Duér - me - te, ni - ñi - to, que ten - go que ha-cer; la -

var tus pa - ña - les, po - ner-me a co - ser u -

na ca - mi - si - ta que te has de po - ner el

día de tu san - to, Se - ñor San Mi - guel.

Go to sleep, dear child,
I have a lot to do;
I must wash all your diapers
And sew a shirt, too.
You'll wear it on your saint's day,
Saint Michael's Day, it's true,
So go to sleep, my dear child,
Go to sleep, do.

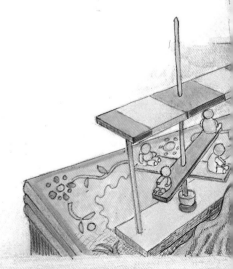

28

De colores   Oh, the Colors

Con alegría   Joyfully

De ____ co - lo - res, ____ de co - lo - res se vis - ten los

cam-pos en la pri - ma - ve - ra; _____ de ____ co -

lo - res, ___ de co - lo - res son los pa - ja - ri - llos que vie-nen de a -

fue - ra; _____ de ____ co - lo - res, ____ de co -

lo - res es el ar - co i - ris que ve - mos lu - cir; ____ y por

e - so los gran-des a - mo-res, de mu-chos co - lo - res me gus-tan a

mí.   mí. _____ Y por e - so los gran - des a -

mo - res, de mu - chos co - lo - res me gus - tan a mí.

Canta el gallo, canta el gallo
con el kiri, kiri, kiri, kiri, kiri;
la gallina, la gallina
con el cara, cara, cara, cara, cara;
los polluelos, los polluelos
con el pío, pío, pío, pío, pi;
y por eso los grandes amores
de muchos colores me gustan a mí.
Y por eso los grandes amores
de muchos colores me gustan a mí.

Oh, the colors! Oh, the colors appear
In the fields every year in the spring.
Oh, the colors! Oh, the colors appear
On the birds that come here to sing.
Oh, the colors! Oh, the colors appear
In the rainbow that shines high above.

And the colors are so bright and pretty
And make me so happy,
They fill me with love.

Oh, the rooster! He says cock-cock-a-doodle,
Doo-doo, cock-a-doodle: good day!
Oh, the hen! She says cack-cackle-cack,
Cackle-cack-cackle-cackle: let's play!
Oh, the chicks! They say peep-peep-peep,
Peep-peep-peep-peep to the birds up above.
And the world is so bright and so pretty
And makes me so happy,
It fills me with love.

Nota de las autoras   Authors' Note

Cuando éramos muy jóvenes nuestras familias se mudaron de los Estados Unidos a México y Chile. Asimilamos rápidamente las canciones y poemas infantiles que nos enseñaban en el aula de la escuela. Por la tarde regresábamos a nuestras casas y sin ningún esfuerzo, se los recitábamos a nuestros admirados padres, mientras que ellos batallaban llenos de frustración con las sempieternas grabaciones Berlitz. Con el tiempo todos aprendimos español, pero fueron la poesía y la música las que mejor nos proporcionaron un acceso directo a las calidades vibrantes, musicales y dramáticas de la lengua.

Las rimas que aprendimos hace tantos años nos han acompañado durante toda la vida. Hoy día, las dos somos madres, profesoras y grandes admiradoras de la buena poesía escrita para los niños en cualquier lengua. Por eso, hemos preparado esta colección, para establecer un vínculo seguro entre aquellos adultos y niños que quieran aprender y practicar ambas lenguas juntos.

Estas canciones son tesoros nacionales y fuentes de cultura y tradición que son y seguirán siendo transmitidos de generación a generación.

¡Coge a tus niños en brazos para que muy cerquita juntos canten estas canciones! Todas contienen dentro de sí ese espíritu universal que está en todas partes, a través del cual la familia comparte amor, a la vez que con gran alegría aprende y disfruta como nosotras lo hicimos.

When we were very young, our families moved from the United States to Mexico and Chile. We quickly absorbed the chants and verses we heard in the classroom and on the playground. We headed home to recite and sing effortlessly in Spanish for our proud yet flabbergasted parents, struggling themselves with Berlitz recordings. Though we all learned Spanish, poetry and song afforded us children immediate access into the vibrant, musical, and dramatic qualities of the language.

The rhymes we learned so many years ago have accompanied us through life. Today we are both mothers, teachers, and lovers of good poetry for children in any language. We have compiled this collection for all adults and children who wish to learn and practice both languages together.

These songs are national treasures—repositories of culture and tradition that should continue to be passed from generation to generation.

So hold your child close, and recite and sing these verses together. They carry with them the love between children and parents everywhere, sharing, learning, and laughing together.